This book belongs to

Useful words

(in the order they appear in this book)

jumble

boots

hat

dress

raincoat

cardigan

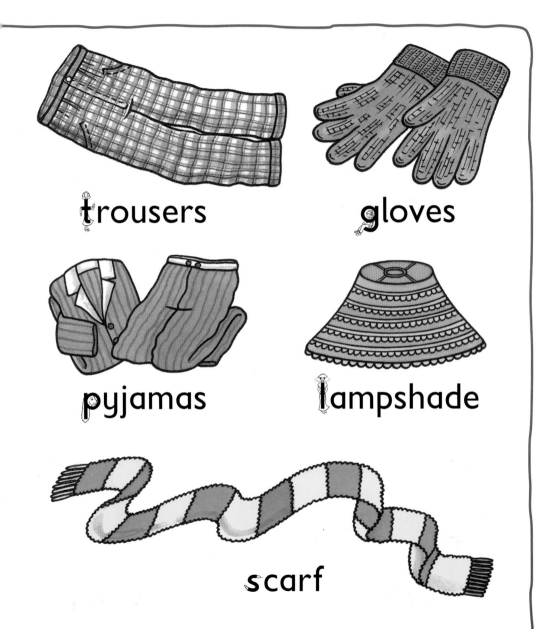

trousers

gloves

pyjamas

lampshade

scarf

Jumping Jim's Jumble sale

Katie Carr

Jumping Jim is having a
jumble sale today.

What can you find at
the jumble sale?

Can you find some boots,
some blue boots ...

for Bouncy Ben?

Can you find a hat,
a hairy hat …

for the Hat Man?

Can you find a dress,
a dancing dress …

for Dippy Duck?

Can you find a raincoat,
a red raincoat …

for Robber Red?

Can you find a cardigan,
a cosy cardigan ...

for Clever Cat?

Can you find some trousers,
some tartan trousers ...

for Ticking Tess?

Can you find some gloves,
some green gloves ...

for Golden Girl?

Can you find some pyjamas,
some purple pyjamas …

for Poor Peter?

Can you find a lampshade,
a lacy lampshade …

for Lamp Lady?

Can you find a scarf,
a soft scarf ...

for Sammy Snake?

But what about Jumping Jim?
Can you find anything for him?

The Letterlanders

| Annie Apple | Bouncy Ben | Clever Cat | Dippy Duck | Eddy Elephant | Fireman Fred | Golden Girl |

| Hairy Hat Man | Impy Ink | Jumping Jim | Kicking King | Lucy Lamp Lady | Munching Mike |

| Naughty Nick | Oscar Orange | Poor Peter | Quarrelsome Queen | Robber Red | Sammy Snake | Ticking Tess |

| Uppy Umbrella | Vase of Violets | Wicked Water Witch | Max and Maxine | Yellow Yo-yo Man | Zig Zag Zebra |

Published by Collins Educational
An imprint of HarperCollins*Publishers* Ltd
77-85 Fulham Palace Road
London W6 8JB

www.**fire**and**water**.com
Visit the book lover's website

First published 1998
Reprinted 2000

ISBN 0 00 303406 2

LETTERLAND® is a registered trademark of Lyn Wendon.

The author asserts the moral right to be identified as the author of this work.

British Library Cataloguing in Publication Data
A catalogue record for this book is available from the British Library.

Written by Katie Carr
Illustrated by Anna Jupp
Designed by Michael Sturley and Sally Boothroyd
Consultant: Lyn Wendon, originator of Letterland

Printed by Printing Express, Hong Kong

Letterland®

Letterland At Home is a range of books, cassettes and flashcards that uses a fun approach to help children to read and write. Three colour-coded Stages will help you to choose the books that are right for your child.

Stage 1

Stage 2

Available from all good bookshops.

For an information leaflet about Letterland call 020 8307 4052.

Stage 3

For younger children, a colourful range of first skills activity books has been developed.